Ride With
The Loomis Gang

Ride With
The Loomis Gang

E. Fuller Torrey, M.D.

With illustrations by
John Mahaffy

North Country Books
Utica, New York

RIDE WITH THE LOOMIS GANG

An adaptation of
Frontier Justice: The Rise and Fall of the Loomis Gang
for young readers

Second Printing 2006

ISBN 0-925168-56-4

Library of Congress Cataloging-in-Publication Data

Torrey, E. Fuller (Edwin Fuller), 1937 -
    Ride with the Loomis gang / by E. Fuller Torrey
        p.   cm.
    Adaptation of the author's Frontier justice: the rise and fall of the
Loomis gang.
    Summary: An account of the gang which terrorized central New York
during the mid-1800's and at the peak of its activities consisted of over
200 members throughout the state.
    ISBN 0-925168-56-4 (alk. paper)
    1. Gangs—New York (State)—History—19th Century—Juvenile
literature. 2. Loomis family—Juvenile literature. 3. Criminals—New
York (State)—Oneida County—Biography—Juvenile literature. [1.
Gangs. 2. Loomis family. 3. Criminals.]
I. Torrey, E. Fuller (Edwin Fuller), 1937- Frontier justice. II. Title.
HV6452.N7T67   1996
364.1'06'609747—dc20   96-8217
                                                            CIP
                                                            AC

North Country Books, Inc.
311 Turner Street
Utica, New York 13501
ncbooks@adelphia.net

Dedication

To my grandson, Lucas Alan Anderson,
who soon will be able to read this book.

Contents

Acknowledgments

I am deeply indebted to the work of George W. Walter who researched the Loomis gang from 1930 to 1953. When he died in 1972 he left behind an important collection of Loomis information. Many people assisted me in locating historical data including Russell Hubbard and the staff of the Madison County Historical Society; the staffs of the Oneida Historical Society and Utica Public Library; Ms. Linda Hazelden and Ms. Philippa S. Brown of the Waterville Historical Society and Ms. Wendy Sexton of the Waterville Public Library; E. Stevens Wright of the Onondaga Historical Association; Ms. Betty Smith of the Susquehanna County Historical Society; the staffs of the New York State Historical Association, Rome Historical Society, Cherry Valley Museum, Cornell University Library, and Syracuse University Library; Frank K. Lorenz and Prof. David Ellis of Hamilton College; Howard D. Williams of Hamilton; Judge John J. Walsh of Utica; and the staff of the Library of Congress in Washington. Ms. Lewis and Mr. Engel of the Mohawk Valley Psychiatric Center located the original psychiatric records of Gerrit Smith.

I am also grateful to the Syracuse University Press for permission to quote from H. F. Jackson and T. R. O'Donnell's *Back Home in Oneida: Hermon Clarke and His Letters.*

A draft of this book was read by Daniel Engelstad, Ariel Goldberg, Tessa Hirsch and Laura Myhr who provided me with useful suggestions from the point of view of 4th to 7th graders. I am grateful for their help.

Ms. Judy Miller contributed excellent editing and typing. Ms. Sheila Orlin and North Country Books kindly encouraged the development of the book and made sure it had a good home. And my wife, Barbara, encouraged me to think like a child again.

Lewis

Camden

Hastings
Center

Oswego County

Oneida Lake

Higginsville

Erie Canal

Syracuse

Chittenango

Oneida

Oneida
Castle

Canastota

Oneida
Reservation

Onondaga County

Stockbridge

Peterboro

Cazenovia

Morrisville

Madison

Madison County

Hamilton

Cortland County

De Ruyter

Chenango County

Smyrna

The Loomis Empire

Herkimer County

da County

Rome/Ft. Stamwix

Whitesboro

Westmoreland

Utica

New Hartford

Clinton

Washington Mills

Chadwicks

Ilion

Herkimer

Erie Canal

Stanwix Treaty Line

boro

Brotherton

Waterville

Sangerfield

LOOMIS FARM

Bridgewater

Richfield Springs

North Brookfield

Springfield Center

ubbardsville

Brookfield

Leonardsville

Cherry Valley

Otsego County

burne

Edmeston

Burlington

Cooperstown

Major Characters

George Loomis, the father, born in 1779.

Rhoda Loomis, the mother, born in 1793.

  Their children:

    Calista, born in 1817.

    Bill, born in 1819.

    Cornelia, born in 1821.

    Wash, born in 1823.

    Grove, born in 1825.

    Lucia, born in 1828.

    Wheeler, born in 1831.

    Charlotte, born in 1832.

    Plumb, born in 1834.

    Denio, born in 1836.

James Filkins, constable.

Roscoe Conkling, Utica lawyer and politician.

W.J. Bissell, shopkeeper in Waterville.

Hermon Clarke, clerk in Bissell's store who joined the Union Army.

Gerrit Smith, wealthy landowner in Peterboro who worked to obtain the freedom of the slaves.

Prologue

This is the story of the Loomis Gang, a family outlaw gang that terrorized New York State for twenty years in the middle of the last century. Their headquarters was at the family farm near Sangerfield in Madison County, New York, but their stealing and other illegal activities extended from the Finger Lakes in the western part of New York State to the Vermont border in the east, and from Watertown in the northern New York into Pennsylvania to the south.

At the peak of their activities, in the early 1860s, the gang consisted of at least 200 members who lived in towns spread across New York State. The Loomis Gang leaders, however, were almost all members of the Loomis family. The Loomis Gang was well known to everyone who lived within the territory they controlled and was regularly written about in newspapers in the surrounding towns and in New York City. In 1865 the New York State Legislature ordered a special report on the Loomis Gang, and in 1866 a journal in London, England, published an article about them entitled "Crime in the State of New York."

This is a true story of the gang's activities. All the information in the book is taken from newspapers of that period and from a book by George W. Walter, *The Loomis Gang*, published in 1953. All quotations in this book are taken from those sources. For a few years it looked as though nothing could stop the Loomis Gang and that they would go on robbing and stealing forever. That was before . . . but that's getting ahead of the story.

Chapter 1

How to Steal Muffs and Horses

The education of the ten children in the Loomis family was most unusual, for they were taught by their mother and father to steal things. As Wash Loomis later explained to a friend: "We sometimes traded little things like boys do, and learned quickly to deceive and cheat. Mother smiled approval when she learned of what we did and told us not to get caught nor to allow anyone to get the better of us. We were always supposed to seize the advantage. When we stole little things, Mother approved."

The Loomis family lived in a large farmhouse on a hillside overlooking Nine Mile Swamp, south of Sangerfield and Waterville in central New York. The house, which had seven bedrooms, two stairways and two kitchens, had been specially built by the Loomises and had concealed spaces, false floors and double-panelled walls. These spaces were used to hide stolen goods, or even people who were being sought by the law. On many occasions sheriffs and other officers of the law searched the Loomis house looking for stolen goods or gang members suspected of being in the house, yet as often as not the sheriffs came away empty-handed because the stolen goods and gang members were well hidden.

The Loomis children were taught how to read and write as well as how to steal. In fact they were among the best educated children in the area. They all attended the local one-room schoolhouse in Tinker Hollow, down the road from their farm. And in the evenings Mrs. Loomis often read them stories, such as *The Last of the Mohicans*, which had been written by James Fenimore Cooper, who lived in nearby Cooperstown. When the four Loomis daughters—Calista, Cornelia, Lucia, and Charlotte—were older, they attended private schools for young women in nearby Whitestown and Clinton. Charlotte and Lucia also became skilled at playing the piano. And all four girls, just like their brothers, became skilled at stealing.

The fact that the Loomis daughters were taught to steal, just like the Loomis sons, was especially unusual for that period. In the early 1800s women were believed to be inferior to men. Wives and children were considered to be owned by the man who was the head of the household. Women had almost no legal rights, and in fact they were not allowed to vote until 1920, almost one hundred years after our story. At the time the Loomis children were growing up, even prizes that women won for needlework at the Oneida County Fair were awarded to the male head of the household, rather than to the woman directly, because the woman was considered to be the property of the man.

Shoplifting was one of the favorite methods used by the Loomis girls for stealing. Women's skirts in those days were very full and came down to their ankles. It was possible, therefore, to hide a large variety of items under a skirt and walk out of the store. Another favorite trick used by the Loomis girls was to steal fur muffs. All women carried muffs in the winter to keep their hands warm when riding in horse-drawn sleighs, a common means of transportation back then. Good muffs were expensive to buy and so they were desirable to steal.

The Loomis girls' usual method of stealing muffs was to slip them onto their legs, where they were covered by their long skirts and thus the muffs could not be seen. Sometimes two of the girls would go into a store together and, while one girl distracted the shopkeeper in one part of the store, the other girl would slip two or three muffs onto her legs under her skirt.

On other occasions the Loomis girls would go to parties in nearby towns, and at the end of the parties several other girls would not be able to find their muffs. One night, after this had been repeated at several parties, the Loomis girls got caught. This is the way it was described in a newspaper account from that period:

"When the party broke up around two in the morning, a number of the girls couldn't find their muffs. They hunted high and low. Finally one girl, a little older and bolder than the rest, went around and pulled up the dress and petticoat of one of the Loomis girls and beheld that she had four or five muffs on each leg. She shoved her over backwards on the bed and called two girls to hold her hands and other girls held her feet so she couldn't kick. They disrobed her of the muffs and then led her to the door and shoved her out. That ended the Loomis girls going to any more parties."

While the Loomis girls were stealing clothing and muffs, the six Loomis boys were learning to steal almost anything they could carry home. Bill was the oldest, but he was a follower. Wash, the next oldest, was the leader of the Loomis boys from the time he was a young man, and he was supported by Grove, who was two years younger. Wheeler, Plumb and Denio were the youngest, and as children, they mostly did what Wash and Grove told them to do.

As children, the Loomis boys stole small items from stores. As they grew older they stole things from the nearby farmyards, like chickens, lambs, or clothes that had been hung out to dry. Mrs. Loomis encouraged her sons in these activities. According to a newspaper account Mrs. Loomis would tell her sons: "Now don't you come back without stealing something, if it's nothing but a jackknife." Wash was especially skilled at stealing, and as he got older he stole larger items and often broke into homes or stores when nobody was there.

Grove Loomis liked horses and was said to be a very good judge of them. His father taught him how to steal them. Mr. Loomis had himself been stealing horses since he was a young man, and he taught Grove and his other sons everything he knew. Mr. Loomis, with Grove by his side, would often ride the roads throughout central New York looking for horses. When they spotted what looked like a fine one, Mr. Loomis would approach the farmer who owned it and, pretending to be a horse buyer, ask him how much he would sell it for. This gave Mr. Loomis an opportunity to look the horse over closely. Often the farmer said he would not sell it, or if he did quote a price, Mr. Loomis would say that the price was too high.

Late at night, within two or three weeks of when the horse had been examined, Mr. Loomis would return and steal the horse. As his sons grew older they would go with their father on these trips. Mr. Loomis often wrapped burlap around the horses' hooves so that they would not make loud noises on the road as he led them away. Mr. Loomis had also learned how to use dyes to change the coloring of a horse and how to use something very hot that made white markings on the horse. By skillfully doing this, Mr. Loomis could change the appearance of a horse so much that sometimes even its owner would not recognize it. Good horses were very valuable in the nineteenth century, and it was easy to find a buyer for them. On at least one occasion the Loomises sold a horse back to the man from whom it had been stolen, because the horse's color and markings had been changed so much that the owner did not realize that he was buying back his own horse.

In addition to learning how to read, write and steal, the Loomis children were expected to do their share of chores on the farm. The girls helped feed the chickens and learned how to bake bread using a Dutch oven that was buried in burning coals in the large fireplace. In the evening Mrs. Loomis showed them how to spin, weave and knit. The boys led the cows to the upper meadow to pasture in the morning and returned them to the barn for feeding and milking in the evening. The boys also helped bring water to the house from the well and stacked firewood that had been chopped by their father and by men he hired to help him. The boys learned from their father how to plant corn, pumpkins, beans, potatoes, cabbage and turnips, and how to store some of them in deep holes in the ground so the vegetables could be eaten months later.

In the spring, all the Loomis children helped tap the maple trees to collect the dripping sap that was used to make maple syrup and maple candy. And in the late summer they all helped pick berries, which were made into jams and jellies.

Nobody who knew Mr. and Mrs. Loomis were surprised that they were teaching their children how to steal. Ever since George Loomis had come to Sangerfield in 1802 as a twenty-three-year-old man, his name had been associated with crimes of one kind or another. Despite the fact that he had come from a highly respected and well-to-do family in Connecticut, George Loomis had chosen a life of crime.

One of George Loomis' specialties was counterfeiting money, which was easy to do in the early nineteenth century, because there was no standard currency and each bank made its own paper money. Therefore, the money made by one bank looked different from money made by another bank, and it was relatively easy for counterfeiters to pass their fake bills. George Loomis had been arrested for counterfeiting as early as 1810, when he mistakenly tried to give a counterfeit hundred dollar bill to a law officer in Sangerfield.

Despite his arrest Mr. Loomis did not go to jail. He had learned that many law officers could be bribed with money or gifts, and he used this strategy on many occasions to get charges dropped after he had been arrested. When that strategy failed he threatened to get even with the law officers by burning their barns to the ground, and on several occasions he did so. Therefore, despite many years of counterfeiting, stealing and selling whiskey illegally, George Loomis had spent almost no time in jail for his crimes.

Mrs. Rhoda Loomis had also been involved in illegal activities for many years and had herself been raised in a family in which such activities were the norm. Her father had served time in prison for forgery and selling whiskey illegally, and it was rumored that as a girl Rhoda had helped her father. Rhoda was also highly intelligent, had done well in school, and had even taught school in Utica before she had married George Loomis. Since it was unusual for girls to go to school at all in those days, Rhoda Loomis was among the best educated women in the area in which she lived.

The neighbors of the Loomises often asked each other why George and Rhoda Loomis had chosen to live a life of crime and why they raised their children to be thieves. They noticed that both George and Rhoda liked fine things, and found it easier to steal them than to work for them. And they knew that in Rhoda's case, she had learned her criminal skills from her father. The neighbors also liked to repeat what George Loomis himself often said: "Everybody steals, so why shouldn't I?"

George Loomis was very fond of telling about the Oneida Indians, who once lived on the lands around Sangerfield and Waterville. The Oneidas, along with the Tuscaroras, had been the only two Indian tribes in America who had sided with the Americans in the Revolutionary War. All the others fought for the British in the war.

After the war, as a reward for their support, the Continental Congress in 1784 approved the Treaty of Fort Stanwix, which guaranteed the Oneida Indians six million acres of land. Within two years, however, Governor George Clinton of New York and other government officials pressured the Oneidas to sell some of their land to settlers. Within ten years following the signing of the Treaty of Fort Stanwix, the Oneidas had been pressured into selling 97 percent of their land, some of which was purchased from them illegally. The land around Sangerfield and Waterville, which had been part of the six million acres given to the Oneidas, had been bought from the Oneidas in 1788 for just one-tenth of a cent per acre. Within three years it had been resold for fifty cents an acre, which was 500 times more than the Oneidas had been paid for it. In 1806, when George Loomis bought fifteen acres of it, the price was $14.78 per acre, which was 14,780 times more than the Oneidas had been paid just eighteen years earlier.

George Loomis was fond of telling the story of the sale of the Indian lands, for he said it proved that everyone, even important government officials, was stealing. And if everyone was stealing, why shouldn't he? People listened to George Loomis tell the story, but they told each other that it merely sounded like an excuse. George Loomis and his family stole, said his neighbors, because they liked to steal.

If the Loomis family had confined their illegal activities to stealing, they probably would not be remembered today. But from their earliest years it became clear that the Loomises were capable of more than just stealing. Sometime in the 1830s, when the Loomis children were still young, a tin peddler with a wagon full of shiny tin pots, pans, tools and other household items disappeared while selling his wares house-to-house along the road on which the Loomises lived. Many people suspected that the Loomises were involved in the disappearance and so a search was organized. According to a newspaper account, when the people doing the searching looked around the Loomis farm, "they found a well on the farm filled with stones, and began to clean it out. Halfway down they came to an immense boulder, which had evidently been drawn to the well by a yoke of oxen and rolled in." The boulder could not be moved, and so the bottom of the well could not be searched. Neither the tin peddler nor his wagon was ever found.

From that time on, people who lived near the Loomises became much more wary of them. The Loomis family, it seemed, could not only steal but could murder as well. People who had regarded them merely as a nuisance now looked at them in a different light.

Over the next few years community opposition to the Loomis family began to increase. Each year the citizens of Sangerfield, Waterville and other nearby towns would say more and more often: "Something needs to be done." But most people were afraid to say it very loudly, because if they did their horses would disappear or their barn would mysteriously be burned to the ground.

Meanwhile, the Loomis children were growing into young adulthood, and thefts became more and more common. As a newspaper described it: "Burglaries were of nightly occurrence.

Clotheslines were robbed, farmers lost their sheep and horses, and there was a multitude of petty thefts." Stories were told about secret hiding places in the Loomis home overflowing with stolen goods. For example, one young woman who had been hired to help with the farmwork at the Loomis home told of seeing large pans filled with watches and jewelry hidden beneath the floorboards in the barn. Each year the Loomis family seemed to become richer and richer.

Finally in 1848 people had had enough. On a snowy December afternoon several sleighs filled with armed men drove up the Loomis home and demanded to search it. The house was found to be full of stolen goods, including clothing, furs, buffalo robes, saddles, harnesses and wagon parts. Wash and Bill Loomis were immediately arrested and charged with theft. They were taken to jail but then released on bail to await their trial. Wash avoided going to trial by leaving town and going to California, where the Gold Rush was under way.

It looked as though it might be the end of the Loomis family's stealing. Everyone, except for the Loomises, was happy. In fact, however, it was not the end at all, but merely the beginning.

Chapter 2

The Secret of Nine Mile Swamp

In late 1850, almost two years after Wash Loomis had gone to California, he suddenly reappeared in Sangerfield, riding a golden California mare, smiling, and tipping his hat to the ladies. Word of his return spread quickly, and people reacted with surprise and concern. There had been rumors that Wash had been killed in California in a gunfight, and most people had hoped that those rumors were true.

During Wash's absence the number of thefts and other crimes in central New York had decreased sharply. George Loomis, the father, was becoming increasingly forgetful as he approached seventy years old, and he could no longer organize his family's criminal activities. Rhoda Loomis tried to assume leadership of the family, but the older children paid little attention to their mother as they each went their separate ways. Calista had married a lawyer in Whitesboro, while Bill, Cornelia, Grove, and Lucia were all in their twenties and not about to let their mother tell them what to do. Only the two youngest children, Plumb, age sixteen, and Denio, age fourteen, would still do their mother's bidding. The once-feared Loomis family had become a mere shadow of its former self.

That would all change with Wash's return, for Wash, age twenty-seven, was looked up to by his brothers and sisters. His leadership position was further strengthened three months after his return, when his father died after a short illness. There was now no question about who was in charge of the Loomis family. People in surrounding towns talked nervously about what might happen next.

Wash Loomis immediately went to work to enlarge and modernize the activities of the Loomises. It was the modern era, he said. Words could now travel faster, thanks to the invention of the telegraph by Samuel Morse, who had built the first telegraph machine in nearby Cherry Valley in 1837. Morse had then gone into partnership in 1842 with Ezra Cornell, who had grown up in Madison County, and together they had built telegraph lines between cities and began a company that became known as Western Union. The Loomises could therefore communicate with each other by telegraph within minutes over hundreds of miles, which was a big change from the stagecoach mail system, which had taken many days or even weeks to get a message through.

Transportation had also speeded up. The dirt roads had been improved by laying wooden planks on them so that stagecoaches could travel faster. The Erie Canal had opened in 1825, and twelve years later the Chenango Canal also opened, stretching from Binghamton to Utica, where it joined the Erie Canal. The Chenango Canal passed through the town of Madison, which was just six miles from the Loomis farm. Stolen horses could be driven to the canal, put on boats, and taken all the way to Albany or even New York City to be sold.

The most exciting modern invention, however, was the railroad. The first trains started running between Albany and Syracuse in 1839, and with each passing year more tracks were laid. The railroad between Utica and Rome was especially well known, for it passed over a swampy area. A system was devised to raise the railroad tracks a few feet off the ground. A newspaper likened the train ride over this area to "sailing through the air." It was considered to be so unusual that even the President of the United States, Martin Van Buren, stopped in Utica to try it. The Loomises had close relatives living in Hastings Center, north of Syracuse, and they regularly used the train to go back and forth and to transport stolen goods to sell them in distant towns.

The most important of the Loomises' expanded activities was horse stealing. Wash organized the stealing by area, so that Bill was responsible for the northern area from Rome to Camden and Hastings Center; Grove was responsible for the southern area from Sherburne to Norwich and Binghamton; while Wash himself took responsibility for the eastern area from Cooperstown to Albany and into Vermont, where the Loomises had cousins living. Responsibility for the western area from Syracuse to Auburn and the Finger Lakes was given to Big Bill Rockwell, a well-known horse thief from Moravia who had become a close friend of the Loomises.

The Loomises began stealing more and more horses by recruiting other people to help them. After several horses had been stolen in one area, a string of the stolen horses would be led during the night to the Loomises' farm. Once there the horses were taken down the hill and into Nine Mile Swamp, which was more than a mile wide and contained hidden trails and clearings where the stolen horses were kept until they could be sold. The swamp was impossible to cross unless a person knew the trails; one step in the wrong direction and they would suddenly be in water up to their waist. There were also rumors that there was quicksand in the swamp that would completely swallow a horse and rider in five minutes, never to be seen again. For this reason few people dared to go near Nine Mile Swamp.

The Loomises, however, knew Nine Mile Swamp like the back of their hand, and they used it as their private hiding place. They opened secret trails, cleared some of the solid ground that was hidden in the swamp for pastures, and even built a small barn in which to keep feed for their horses. A book published in 1927 described in detail how the Loomises used Nine Mile Swamp to hide their stolen horses:

"The horses were led into the swamp, each one by a different path, so as to make their tracks confusing. Following an irregular, twisting course, they all converged to one point about two miles from where they entered the swamp. At that point the swamp was almost impassable. There was a sort of an island, comprising about one acre of land, almost entirely surrounded by water, forming a moat. The boys had constructed a temporary bridge, by which the island, as it was known to them, could be reached. The bridge was constructed in such a way that it could be put in place or taken down in an incredibly short time. It was composed of planks which would be hidden in different parts of the swamp when the bridge was not in use. The island itself was fringed in with scrubby trees and underbrush, hiding the interior, which had been cleared off by the boys, completely."

From time to time the Loomises got caught stealing horses. For example, on one occasion Grove Loomis made the mistake of stealing a horse that belonged to young Herbert Throop of Sangerfield. Unknown to Grove, Herbert had taught his horse to do tricks, such as dance, kneel, roll over and play dead. When Herbert Throop's horse was stolen everyone assumed that the Loomises had stolen it. Herbert and his father went directly to the Loomises' farm and demanded the return of their horse. Using dyes and hot potatoes, Grove had already changed the markings on the horse so it looked quite different, but he had not yet taken the horse into the swamp to be hidden there.

The markings didn't fool young Herbert. He went to the Loomises' pasture and called loudly. The horse, with changed markings, immediately trotted over, with Grove insisting that it was his own horse which he had recently bought in Pennsylvania. At that point Herbert Throop ordered the horse to dance, then kneel, roll over and play dead, all of which the horse did without hesitation. Grove Loomis became more and more embarrassed as the horse went through its tricks. When the horse had finished its last trick Grove quickly opened the pasture gate and told Herbert to take his horse home. That horse was never stolen again.

Grove Loomis, who was considered to be an excellent judge of horses, bred them as well as stole them. On one occasion he bred one of the finest horses with a mare owned by a nearby farmer. The resulting offspring was a filly that had a short tail and was named Flora Temple. Grove sold Flora Temple to a horse trainer, who raised her to be a trotter. Flora Temple became a very successful trotter and won almost every race in which she was entered. She became the most famous horse of her time and was even the subject of a song, the "bob-tailed nag" in a song about the Camptown Races: "I'll bet my money on the bob-tailed nag, somebody bet on the bay." For the rest of his life Grove Loomis boasted about his role in the creation of Flora Temple.

Stealing and selling horses was big business in the 1850s, for horses were the most important means of transportation for most people. When other people stole a horse for them, the Loomises paid them fifty or one hundred dollars, then the Loomises would sell the horse for two or three times as much. A really fine horse sometimes sold for a thousand dollars or more, and Grove's favorite horse, a Black Hawk stallion, was valued at over six thousand dollars.

As the Loomis horse stealing activity increased, new ways to sell the horses had to be developed. The hidden pastures in Nine Mile Swamp were often filled with over a hundred horses at a time, and newly stolen horses were arriving almost every night. Canal boats were frequently used to ship the horses to Albany and New York, but only so many horses could be shipped that way without arousing too much suspicion. Another way of transporting the horses was to lead lines of them north through Camden and Sacketts Harbor to Cape Vincent, where they could be loaded on boats and taken down the St. Lawrence River to Montreal to be sold there. Other horses were led south into Pennsylvania or east into Vermont, where the Loomises had relatives and friends who would sell them. With each passing month more horse were stolen and sold, and the Loomis family became richer and richer.

Although horse theft was the most important of the Loomises' illegal activities, they in fact stole almost anything they could. And as their network of gang members got bigger, they increasingly used this network to sell the things that had been stolen. For example, a saddle stolen by Big Bill Rockwell in the Finger Lakes region would be brought to the Loomises, then sent to Oriskany Falls, where it would be sold by Julius Glazier, who was also on the Loomises' payroll. Glazier, in turn, would steal some fur robes from a store in Oriskany Falls, and the Loomises would send them to Syracuse to be sold there by John Maxwell. Maxwell would then steal some boxes of new leather boots, which the Loomises would send to Bill Alvord in Madison to sell. The person who did the stealing would be paid by the Loomises, and the person who did the selling would also be paid, but the Loomises always kept some of the profit. In this way, they became more wealthy as they used other people to do the actual stealing for them.

By late 1852, two years after Wash had returned from California, the Loomises' network of accomplices was well developed. To celebrate this, the Loomises asked them all to come to a party, which was held on the top of the hill behind the Loomis home. From that hill, now called Loomis Nob, one can see rich farmland for many miles in all directions. To the east Nine Mile Swamp stretches out, as dark and forbidding today as it was in 1852. Approximately seventy men, many with their wives, gathered to celebrate with the Loomises. One man who passed the Loomis house that day wrote that "the wagons and rigs all headed in toward the house and the horses tied there . . . were just as thick as they could be."

It was a grand party. Tables that had been brought to the hilltop overflowed with food of all kinds. Rum flowed freely. A band, which had been hired for the occasion, played traditional nineteenth century dance tunes, and many people danced.

The Loomis family circulated among their friends, exchanging stories and gossip. Wash Loomis was acknowledged by all to be the leader, with Grove at his side as the second-in-command. What had once been the Loomis family had enlarged and was now the Loomis Gang. The Loomises already controlled illegal activities throughout central New York and were growing stronger with each passing month. Would anyone be able to stop them?

Chapter 3

Tricks and Crimes of the Loomis Gang

Crimes committed by the Loomis Gang increased sharply during the 1850s. At the time of their party in 1852, the Loomises had approximately seventy gang members, but by 1860 they had over two hundred of them. Each additional accomplice meant that more things would be stolen and that the Loomises, who controlled the overall operation, would become richer. Each additional accomplice also meant that more territory could be covered, and by 1860 the Loomis crime empire stretched from the Canadian border to northern Pennsylvania and from the Finger Lakes region into southern Vermont.

Throughout the large territory that the Loomises controlled, they had a network of houses in which gang members could stay when they travelled. This was well described by one man who took a trip with Wash Loomis to find the man's horse, which had been stolen by mistake:

> "We journeyed southward for four days, far into Pennsylvania. Whenever we were hungry or needed a place to spend the night, Wash would stop at some farm or wayside tavern. There was always a table set for us or beds ready for us to sleep in. No one asked either of us any questions, and we did not pay a cent out for the hospitality shown us. I sensed it was all a part of the vast Loomis organization."

Given the number of Loomis Gang members, it was not surprising to find that thefts of all kinds increased each year. Anything that might be sold, no matter how small or how large, was taken by gang members. An article from the newspaper in Madison regarding thefts in that small village provides an idea of how common thefts had become:

"Horses, harnesses, leather boots, shoes, buffalo and wolf robes, cloth, clothing, etc. were taken. Not long ago ladies' underclothes were taken from the yard of Allen Curtis, the same night a small quantity was missed from the yard of John Dye. The next night an attempt was made to enter Mr. Dye's home. A few nights later an attempt was made to pick the lock of Curtis and Dye's carriage house. It failed. On Tuesday night of the fifth, two valuable robes and thirty chickens were taken from Henry Taylor and a piece of cotton cloth from D. Z. Brockett. On Sunday evening of the tenth, a robe was stolen from Rev. C. Swift's carriage while he conducted religious services at the Durfee School House."

Stealing ladies' underclothes from a clothesline was the least of the Loomises' crimes. Increasingly, gang members broke into houses when nobody was at home and stole everything of value they could find. These were years of good crops in central New York and the farmers got high prices for their corn, wheat, oats, and especially their hops, which were widely grown. Farmers had a lot of money, and since many of them did not trust the banks, they hid their money and gold at home instead. This made it comparatively easy for Loomis Gang members, who had only to find the hiding places.

One of the Loomises' tricks for finding the hiding places is illustrated by a story about Wash Loomis, who sometimes pretended that he was a buyer of gold coins. On one occasion Wash went to the house of a farmer who Wash believed had a lot of money, and he told the farmer that he was a buyer of gold coins and would pay very high prices for them. The farmer went to the attic, where his gold and money were hidden, and got out his coins to show Wash. Wash watched where the farmer went, so he learned the farmer's hiding place. When the farmer showed the gold coins to him, Wash made an offer which was much too low and which he knew the farmer would not accept. Wash then left.

Late that night a burglar broke into the attic where the gold and money were hidden. By chance, however, the farmer's son was sleeping in the attic that night and when the burglar saw the boy he fled. The burglar was either Wash Loomis or another gang member who had been told by Wash where to look.

In addition to breaking into houses, Loomis Gang members also broke into stores with increasing frequency. On one occasion in Deansboro, according to a newspaper account, they "knocked off the knob on the safe with a sledge hammer, drilled through the outer wall of the safe door and then blew it open with a charge of gunpowder." On another occasion, on the Waterville-Utica Road, they broke into a factory that made guns and stole fifty-two of them; many of the guns were later found in the Loomis house during a raid by the sheriff.

Guns were just becoming popular among criminals in the 1850s. Twenty years earlier Samuel Colt had developed the revolver, which consisted of six chambers that revolved around a single barrel; these revolvers originally used a ball and gunpowder. In the 1850s bullets replaced the ball and powder, making the revolver much easier to use.

Loomis Gang members were among the first criminals in America to use revolvers on a regular basis. And the results were predictable. A few weeks after the Loomises had stolen the guns from the gun factory, a farmer near Waterville heard thieves breaking into his barn and went out to try and stop them. As he entered the barn he was shot by the thieves, who were said to be members of the Loomis Gang. That farmer lived, but another farmer near Morrisville a few weeks later was not as lucky and was killed trying to stop a burglary of his barn. The Loomis Gang was suspected of having committed the crime, but it could never be proven.

In addition to their thefts, the Loomis Gang also continued distributing counterfeit money during the 1850s. Bill Loomis was especially good at this. For example, he supplied counterfeit money to a storekeeper who gave the worthless money to customers when giving change; Bill and the storekeeper then split the profits.

The Loomises also used counterfeit money to pay for things. For example, on one occasion Cornelia and Charlotte Loomis wanted to buy two oxen from a farmer in Brookfield. The price asked by the farmer was high—three hundred and sixty dollars— but Cornelia and Charlotte agreed. They then asked the farmer for a yoke to use to drive the oxen to their home, but the farmer insisted that the Loomis girls pay another two dollars for the yoke. When the farmer took the money to the bank he found that only the final two dollars were real money, and all the rest was counterfeit.

As the Loomis Gang grew larger and larger, the Loomises worried more about gang members who might betray them and go to the sheriff. When the gang had been small and consisted only of Loomis family members and a few friends, this had not been a problem. But by the late 1850s the gang had grown to over two hundred members.

The Loomises used several means to keep gang members in line. On one occasion, for example, a gang member threatened to expose the Loomises and then left for Utica. When he arrived there he was immediately arrested and charged with theft. Before he had left the Loomis farm, the Loomises had hidden a watch in his pack, then telegraphed the sheriff in Utica and notified him about the "stolen" watch. On another occasion a gang member complained that the Loomises owed him more money than he had been paid. With the Loomises' permission, the man took a horse and rode to Clinton, where he was arrested. The Loomises had accused the man of stealing their horse and had asked the sheriff to arrest him. The Loomises offered to drop the theft charges if the man agreed to forget the money he was owed, which he did.

The most extreme means used by the Loomises to keep gang members in line was murder. Once a gang member complained loudly that the Loomises had cheated him out of some money, and he said that he was going to tell the sheriff about their criminal activities. Wash calmed the man down and assured him that the debt would be settled. While they were waiting, Wash asked the man, along with several other members, to help cut hay. The cutting of hay in those days was done with long scythes, and each man carried one as they climbed the hill behind the Loomis home to the upper meadow.

Suddenly a scythe flashed through the air and hit the man in the middle of his stomach. Within minutes he had died. Everybody who was there said the man had stumbled and fallen on his own scythe, and it certainly was a shame. Nobody else, of course, believed the story. But after that, members of the Loomis Gang thought long and hard before complaining.

Thefts, counterfeiting, arson, murder—there appeared to be no end to the Loomises' criminal activities. Each year the gang grew larger and their crimes increased. Would it ever end?

By the late 1850s most of the citizens of central New York were growing tired of the Loomis Gang's crimes. Increasingly, voices were raised saying that something should be done. One of the loudest of these voices was that of W. J. Bissell, who ran the general store in Waterville. The store sold seeds, tools, food, medicines, cigars and candy—everything a family needed, except clothes. It was a popular gathering place for the people in Waterville and for farmers who lived nearby, and everyone nodded in agreement as Mr. Bissell set forth his none-too-kind opinion of the Loomises and what should be done with them.

Mr. Bissell's favorite solution for the Loomises was "the California solution." This referred to events in San Francisco, California, in 1851, when the city was taken over by criminals and the sheriff seemed helpless to stop them. A group of citizens got together and formed the San Francisco Vigilance Committee. This committee immediately arrested thirty-two of the worst criminals, publicly hung four of them, and expelled the others from the city forever. The citizens in effect took the law into their own hands and did what the sheriff had not been able to do. Six thousand citizens of San Francisco signed petitions in support of the actions of the Vigilance Committee. Many newspapers in the east, including those in New York and Boston, expressed support for the action of the Vigilance Committee.

Another important voice being raised in opposition to the Loomis Gang was that of Roscoe Conkling. In 1850 Conkling had been the District Attorney for Oneida County when Bill Loomis had been brought to trial for theft. Conkling worked hard and got a conviction. Bill Loomis was fined and sent to jail for two months, the first member of the Loomis Gang to spend more than a few days in jail. The Loomises vowed to get revenge on Conkling, and when Conkling came up for reelection for the District Attorney position, the Loomises worked hard to persuade people to vote against him. Conkling lost that election and blamed his loss on the Loomises. He was then elected Mayor of Utica, and in 1858 was elected to the United States Congress. By 1860 he was a powerful political figure. And he remembered the Loomises well and what they had done to defeat him.

A third voice being raised against the Loomises in the 1850s was Jim Filkins. Filkins was a short, heavy man with sandy hair and a beard, who worked as a blacksmith in North Brookfield, a village across Nine Mile Swamp from the Loomises. He was a year younger than Wash and a year older than Grove, and for reasons nobody understood Filkins hated the Loomises. Some people said that Filkins himself had been a member of the Loomis Gang but had had a disagreement with them. Others said that the bad feelings between Filkins and the Loomis boys were caused by a young woman who had turned Filkins down in favor of Wash. Whatever the cause, Jim Filkins was the loudest and most consistent critic of the Loomises.

Although nobody was aware of it at the time, important events were taking place only fifteen miles from the Loomis farm that would also play a major role in the downfall of the gang. These events, which would lead to the Civil War, were taking place in Peterboro, in Madison County, at the large home of Gerrit Smith, a very wealthy landowner. Smith was one of the leading voices in the North urging that the slaves in the South be freed. His home in Peterboro was a stop on the Underground Railway, by which slaves in the South ran away and were helped to escape to Canada, where they would be safe. Many important people who were also working to free the slaves were regular visitors to Gerrit Smith's home, including Horace Greeley, Frederick Douglass, Henry Ward Beecher, Henry Stanton, and Elizabeth Cady Stanton, who later became well known for her role in promoting equality for women.

But the regular visitor to Gerrit Smith's home who was to become the most famous was John Brown. He had first visited in 1848, when he told Gerrit Smith about his plan to free the slaves by getting them to rise up and fight. Smith became a strong supporter of John Brown's plans and contributed large amounts of money to help Brown. By 1856, when John Brown was in Kansas trying to free some slaves, Gerrit Smith had become Brown's most important financial supporter. Brown was, by then, well known as a troublemaker, and while he was in Kansas, President Buchanan offered a reward of two hundred and fifty dollars for Brown's capture. As an insult to the president, John Brown then publicly offered a reward of two dollars and fifty cents for the capture of President Buchanan.

The final planning of John Brown's raid on Harper's Ferry in West Virginia took place in February 1858 in Gerrit Smith's home in Peterboro. Gerrit Smith contributed most of the money for the raid. Of course nobody else living in Peterboro, Waterville, Sangerfield, or the other surrounding towns, knew what was taking place at that time, but they would all be strongly affected by that decision. The raid had to be delayed for over a year for various reasons, but finally on October 16, 1859, it took place. Ten of John Brown's sixteen troops were killed in the raid, and John Brown was publicly hung one month later. The raid became, in effect, the beginning of the Civil War. Along with the efforts of W. J. Bissel, Roscoe Conkling and Jim Filkins, the events of the Civil War would eventually lead to the end of the Loomis Gang.

Chapter 4

Filkins Challenges the Loomises

The Loomis Gang must have suspected that trouble was coming in 1858 when Jim Filkins was elected constable of Brookfield. A constable is a type of policeman, not as powerful as a sheriff but able to enforce the laws and to make arrests. Since Brookfield was just across Nine Mile Swamp from the Loomis farm, and since everyone knew that Filkins hated the Loomises, trouble was certain.

It did not take Jim Filkins long to begin his duties. At 3 a.m. on July 8, 1858, Filkins and seven deputies surrounded the Loomis farmhouse and called for Plumb Loomis to come out because he was under arrest. Plumb, seeing the house surrounded, jumped out a side window and started running toward Nine Mile Swamp. Filkins was quicker, and he knocked Plumb down and handcuffed him. Filkins and his deputies then took Plumb to the hotel in Brookfield, where they intended to hold him until they could take him before the judge later in the day.

Three hours later Grove Loomis, armed with two revolvers, rode up to the hotel in Brookfield. Waving his guns in the air, he demanded that Filkins immediately set Plumb free and said that Filkins would "suffer the consequences" if he did not. Nobody had previously dared to treat a member of the Loomis family like this, Grove said, and Filkins was not going to do so either. Filkins stood on the hotel porch, waving his own gun in the air, and told Grove that Plumb was going to jail, not home. After Grove rode off, Filkins told a deputy to take Plumb upstairs, handcuff him to a bed, and guard him so that he could not escape.

A short time later noises were heard on the first floor porch roof outside the window where Plumb was being held. Filkins went outside and was just in time to see Plumb jump from the roof onto the back of a waiting horse and ride away with Grove. Outraged, Filkins went upstairs to find out how Plumb had escaped. The deputy who was responsible for Plumb said that he had fallen asleep because he had been up all night and that Plumb had taken that opportunity to release himself from the handcuffs.

Filkins was not easily discouraged. A few nights later he took several deputies and again went to the Loomises to arrest Plumb and Grove. Surrounding the house, Filkins demanded that Plumb and Grove come out. Shortly thereafter the back door of the Loomis home opened and several dogs came rushing out. The dogs started up the hill behind the house, going directly for the deputy who was standing there. The deputy was frightened, and pushed a large stone down the hill to try and scatter the dogs. Down the large stone rolled, missing the dogs completely and instead knocking down another one of the deputies. Wash Loomis stepped outside and laughed at Filkins and the deputy. "What's the matter?" Wash laughed. "Have you and Jim been drinking?" Filkins, completely embarrassed, searched the house for Plumb and Grove Loomis but found neither one.

The reason Plumb and Grove were not found at the Loomis home that night was because they were in Oriskany Falls, hiding in the home of another gang member. Rumors about their hiding place reached Filkins, who asked the Oriskany Falls constable to arrest them. With two deputies he tried to do so, but Plumb and Grove opened fire with their revolvers, slightly wounding one of the deputies. The Loomises had escaped again.

Jim Filkins continued to try to put the Loomises in jail. One week after the Oriskany Falls gun battle, Filkins heard that Plumb and Grove had returned home. Accompanied by several deputies, Filkins approached the Loomis home at dawn in hopes of capturing them still asleep. Wash, Grove and Plumb were already in the barn feeding their horses when they saw Filkins and his deputies coming. Grove Loomis quickly mounted his fastest horse and headed for the fence at full gallop. The horse cleared the fence easily, and Grove was gone. Meanwhile, Plumb started running past the house toward the swamp just as Cornelia Loomis and Adeline Glazier, Plumb's girlfriend, came out the back door. The women knocked down the deputy who was running after Plumb, and then Adeline Glazier proceeded to sit on his head, all one hundred and eighty pounds of her. The other deputies had to come to the deputy's rescue, so that he would not be suffocated. In the meantime, Plumb had fled safely into the swamp.

Rhoda Loomis, her daughters, and the wives and girlfriends of Loomis Gang associates played an important role in Loomis Gang activities. They also did whatever they could to prevent Filkins from arresting the gang members. On one occasion Filkins and his deputies surrounded the Loomis house and demanded that a certain gang member come out to be arrested. Suddenly two Loomis women jumped from a side window, accompanied by a man who was covered with a cape, and the three ran toward the swamp. Filkins and his deputies all ran after them. When they caught up with the three they discovered that the man accompanying the women was not the man they wanted. Taking advantage of the planned diversion, the wanted man had gone out a window on the other side of the house and had safely hidden in the woods. They were rapidly growing tired of Filkins' raids on them. Being awakened in the middle of the night and having to flee to the swamp was not their idea of a good time, especially on cold or rainy nights. They began posting guards around their house so that they would have a warning when Filkins and his men were coming, but that still did not solve the problem. The problem, said the Loomises, was Filkins, and *something* would have to be done about him.

Filkins' raids were a problem by themselves. Even worse, however, was the fact that his raids encouraged other constables and sheriffs in the surrounding communities to also begin raiding the

Loomises. Law officers in almost every village and town in central New York State had warrants for the arrest of one or more Loomis Gang member for crimes they had committed, but until Jim Filkins started going to the Loomis home to arrest gang members, none of the other law officers had dared to do so.

One of these law officers was Fitch Hewitt, a Deputy Sheriff from Madison County, who wanted to arrest Grove Loomis for several counts of stealing horses. In August 1858, Hewitt and several deputies surrounded the Loomis home, then searched it thoroughly, but Grove could not be found. Grove was hiding in the house at the time, however, and he wrote a letter to the *Waterville Times* newspaper making fun of Hewitt:

> "I laughed quite heartily at the temerity of our amiable sheriff, Fitch Hewitt, who looked cautiously into our stove oven the other day, expecting to find me there. I sent word to Fitch that I was baked some years ago, and that if my gun had been loaded I would have peppered him on the spot."

Being made fun of in public made the law officers even more determined to put the Loomis gang behind bars. Looking for Grove on another occasion, Filkins and nine deputies approached the Loomis home one morning just as the sky was growing light. Grove had been warned of the raid and had already left. Plumb Loomis thought it would be a joke on Filkins to pretend that he was Grove, so he dressed in Grove's coat and mounted one of Grove's horses. Seeing a figure that looked like Grove in the early morning light, Filkins and his deputies ordered him to halt, and when he did not, they shot in his direction. Plumb immediately shot back and a gunfight followed. Plumb was injured in the arm by a bullet and his horse was killed, but he got away through the swamp. His wounded arm was cared for by Dr. Medina Preston, who was a doctor in Waterville and Plumb Loomis' first cousin.

Jim Filkins refused to give up. A few months later he surrounded the Loomis home with fifty men and ordered Wash, Grove and Plumb to come out or, he said, he would set the house afire. Seeing the large number of Filkins' men and fearing that Filkins was serious, the three Loomis brothers came out. Immediately each man ran in a different direction. Grove reached the shed, where his prize horse was kept saddled and ready to go. He mounted his horse, then rode directly at the twenty men who were following him, knocking many of them down. With bullets whizzing past him, Grove disappeared down the road. Meanwhile, Plumb had reached the safety of Nine Mile Swamp, where none of the men dared follow. Filkins was left with only Wash, who was handcuffed and put into a wagon to be taken to the Madison County Jail.

The Loomises were only rarely arrested, and when they were, they were almost always able to bribe judges or other officials to immediately release them on bail. It was expected, therefore, that Wash would spend only a few days in jail and would then be released. Three months later he was still there. The Loomises were furious, for none of them had ever been in jail for that long. Feeling sorry for Wash, Mrs. Loomis baked a mince pie and sent it to the jail for him to eat. Beneath the crust of the pie Mrs. Loomis hid two small metal files that Wash could use to saw a hole in the bars on his cell and escape.

However, when the pie arrived at the jail, the jailer, either because he was suspicious or hungry, cut into the pie and discovered the files. According to a newspaper account, the jailer then called out to Wash.

"Say, Wash," he asked, "does your mother put files in all the pies she bakes?"

"What kind of pie?" Wash asked.

"Mince," the jailer replied.

"Yes," Wash said, "she always puts in files when she bakes mince pies."

The jailing of Wash was the final straw for the Loomises, and they decided that it was time to fight back. When he was finally released from jail, Wash, along with Bill and two other gang members, approached Filkins one day and warned him to leave them alone. Filkins, however, told them to get lost and took out more warrants for their arrests.

Since intimidation did not work, the Loomises decided to try another tactic. One day Denio Loomis rode up to Filkins' blacksmith shop, handed him a paper, and told Filkins that *he* was under arrest. The warrant for Filkins arrest had been signed by a corrupt judge who had been bribed by the Loomises. It charged Filkins with assault on the Loomises during one of his raids on their home. At that point Wash, Plumb and Bill Loomis drove up in a wagon with several of Filkins' deputies shackled in the back of the wagon. They were all under arrest, Wash said, and he showed Filkins the warrants for their arrests.

Filkins reluctantly climbed into the back of the wagon to go with the others to a hearing in front of a judge in Madison. Wash started down the road to Madison, but then turned off on the road leading to the Loomis farm. At that point Filkins jumped off the wagon. Grove and Plumb came toward him with clubs, but Filkins pulled out a revolver he had hidden in his boot and threatened to shoot them. Wash thereupon decided to go to Madison as agreed, where the judge immediately released Filkins and his men.

That evening there was a knock on Filkins' door. When he opened the door Wash, Plumb, Denio and two other gang members pushed into the room, knocked Filkins to the floor, and handcuffed him while his wife and children screamed in terror. The Loomises then dumped Filkins into the back of a wagon and drove away. They drove several hours north to Higginsville, where Bill Loomis was living and where another corrupt judge they had bribed had signed a warrant for Filkins' arrest.

The next morning Filkins and the Loomises entered the judge's courtroom. The Loomises' plan was to put Filkins in jail and leave him there for as long as possible. It looked to the Loomises as if their plan was going to work, but suddenly a group of men burst into the courtroom with guns drawn. They were Filkins' deputies, who had learned where the Loomises had taken Filkins and had ridden most of the night to get to Higginsville. Filkins should immediately be released on bail, the men argued, and they waved their guns in the air to emphasize their point. The judge looked at the men, then at the Loomises, and agreed to bail, which was immediately paid and Filkins was set free.

The Loomises were not yet ready to give up in their attempt to put Filkins in jail. Once more they persuaded a judge to sign an order for his arrest on charges of assault, and Filkins was brought to trial in Madison County. The Loomises arranged for the prosecutor in the case to be David Mitchell, known both for his long hair and sympathy to the Loomises. Filkins realized that he was in trouble, so he asked Roscoe Conkling, who strongly disliked the Loomises, to defend him. Conkling was then a congressman, but he still practiced law when Congress was not in session.

The trial of Jim Filkins for assaulting the Loomises drew a full house to the Madison County Courthouse in Morrisville. David Mitchell claimed that the Loomises were "a noble people incapable of crime who were continually being persecuted" by Filkins. Many spectators and members of the jury laughed at this. When his turn came, Roscoe Conkling said that Filkins was the only law official who had had the courage to stand up to the Loomises and that he should be found not guilty of assault. The jury agreed with Conkling, and all charges against Filkins were dismissed. After the verdict was announced Conkling said: "We have met the 'lion of Madison County,' the Honorable Mr. Mitchell. He has shaken his mane and thrashed his tail, but all of his words were to no avail."

Month after month the battle between Jim Filkins and the Loomises went on. Despite Filkins' courageous efforts, the thefts and other criminal activities of the Loomis Gang continued. For example, within a single month in 1861 newspapers listed the robbing of Mr. Waldo on a street in Waterville; the burglary of Mr. Steele's home in Bridgewater with the loss of two thousand five hundred dollars; the burglary of Judge Crandell's office and home in Brookfield, during which the thieves even took Judge Crandell's watch from next to his bed as he slept, and the robbery of Mr. Cole in Deansboro of almost two thousand dollars during which he was beaten unconscious. Burglaries, robberies and horse thefts had become a regular occurrence in every town and village in central New York State, and there was no question in anybody's mind who was responsible.

Jim Filkins was slowing the Loomises down, however, and his constant raids on their home became more and more troublesome for them. They had threatened and tried to intimidate him, and that had not worked. They had tried to get him put in jail, and that had not worked. Finally, in early 1862 the Loomises found a way to get rid of Jim Filkins.

Filkins had been elected constable of North Brookfield, and as such, he was up for reelection in 1862. The Loomises decided to get rid of Filkins by getting him defeated in the election. They threatened many people in North Brookfield, telling them that if they voted for Filkins their barns would be burned. Other people were bribed by the Loomises to vote against him. When election day came and the votes were counted, Jim Filkins had lost the election by three votes. He was no longer the constable and so he could no longer bother the Loomises. The Loomis Gang celebrated their victory. They had finally gotten rid of Jim Filkins. Or had they?

Chapter 5

A Visit in the Night

The citizens of the villages around North Brookfield were shocked when they learned that Jim Filkins had been defeated in his re-election as constable. Filkins was the only man who had dared challenge the Loomis Gang. He was completely honest, which was relatively uncommon among law officers in those days, and was one of the reasons why the Loomis Gang was so successful. Many constables, sheriffs, judges and district attorneys were suspected of being corrupt and of accepting money as bribes.

Such corruption was well known in cities such as New York City. In the eighteen fifties, at the same time as the Loomis Gang was becoming increasingly well known in central New York State, gangs of criminals in New York City were terrorizing city residents. The gangs had names such as the Plug Uglies and the Dead Rabbits. Sometimes the gangs fought each other, and when they did, members of the Dead Rabbits gang would actually carry dead rabbits on the end of spears into the battle.

New York City was also well known for its corrupt politicians, such as William "Boss" Tweed. On one occasion, Tweed purchased three hundred park benches at five dollars each from one branch of the city government, then sold them at six hundred dollars each to another branch of the city government. The Chief of Police in New York City was also known to be corrupt, and with bribes he took from criminals, he built a twenty-three-room mansion on a three-thousand-acre estate.

Corruption among law officers in the small towns of central

New York was also common although less publicized. It is not possible to say precisely how many constables, sheriffs, judges, and district attorneys were on the Loomis Gang's payroll, but it was probably at least one-third, and perhaps as many as one-half, of them. They helped the Loomises for one of three reasons.

The first, and most important reason, was money. The Loomises spent much of their money paying bribes to law officers. Many of these officers probably received a monthly payment from the Loomises. In exchange, they would drop charges brought against the Loomises by Filkins or others, set a minimum bail when the Loomises were arrested, and set minimum punishments when they were convicted of crimes. Rather than sending a Loomis Gang member who had been convicted of a crime to jail, a judge would often have them pay a fine instead.

A second reason why many law officers cooperated with the Loomises was that the Loomises could do them favors. An example of this was Charles Mason, who was first the district attorney and then a judge in Madison County. One evening Mason's wife went to a wedding in the town of Hamilton where her watch, a valuable family heirloom, was stolen from her purse. Mr. Mason let everyone know how much they would like the watch back because it meant so much to his wife. Two days later the watch mysteriously appeared on the Mason's front porch. The Masons and everybody else knew that it had been returned by the Loomises, and thereafter Mr. Mason was helpful to the Loomises whenever he could be.

Another kind of favor the Loomises could do was to help elected officials, such as constables, sheriffs, or district attorneys, get re-elected. Because the Loomis criminal network was so wide, they controlled many votes, and in a close election these votes could make the difference between winning and losing. Roscoe Conkling learned this when he lost the election as Oneida County District Attorney, and Jim Filkins learned this when he lost the election as constable of North Brookfield.

The final reason why many law officers cooperated with the

Loomises was that they were frightened of them. When a member of the Loomis Gang threatened to burn your barn, more often than not it happened. A good example of what could happen if you did not cooperate with the Loomises took place in Montrose, Pennsylvania, when a member of the Loomis Gang was jailed for horse theft. Grove Loomis went to Montrose claiming that the man was innocent, and threatened the sheriff with consequences if he did not release him. Grove said that he would make Montrose "pay well for every day" his friend was kept in jail. The sheriff kept the man in jail, and a few days after he had finally been released a terrible fire destroyed many of the buildings in the center of town.

There are many stories about law officers helping the Loomis Gang. District Attorney Hiram T. Jenkins reduced or dropped charges against the Loomises numerous times and almost certainly was on their payroll. The Loomises' influence on law officers was not only in Oneida and Madison Counties, however, but extended all over New York State and even into Pennsylvania, Vermont, and across the Canadian border into Ontario. On one occasion, when Laverne Beebe, a gang member, was arrested in Ontario, Jim Filkins got an agreement from the local Ontario law officers that they would keep Beebe in jail for eight weeks while Filkins got papers approved by which Beebe could be returned to Oneida County to stand trial. Less than three weeks later Beebe was released by Ontario law officers. Filkins and others strongly suspected that the law officers had been bribed by the Loomises.

Another example of the Loomises' influence on law officers came to light in Oswego. A man and his wife who lived there and who had been members of the Loomis Gang became very angry when their daughter ran off with a member of the gang. The couple started talking publicly about the Loomis Gang's activities and threatened to expose them if their daughter was not sent back home. The Loomises bribed the local judge in Oswego and arranged to have the couple arrested and charged with theft. Rather than bringing them to trial, however, the judge put them in jail and left them there. They had been in jail for a year and a half when the situation was discovered by New York State officials.

Frequently, law officers who had been bribed by the Loomises could not appear to be openly helping them but did so more secretly. An example of this kind of help took place in 1861 in Oneida. Hiram T. Jenkins, who was District Attorney for Oneida County, lived in Oneida and had an office in a separate building in his yard. A key for the door of his office hung nearby. One night somebody who knew where the key was hanging entered his office and removed legal papers that concerned thirty-eight separate crimes the Loomises had committed. Because the papers were stolen, Jenkins said he would have to drop all the charges against the Loomises. Most people believed that Jenkins had told Wash Loomis where the key for the office was hanging and which papers to take.

The best known example of a law officer cooperating with the Loomises was Jarius H. Munger, a District Attorney for Oneida County. Grove Loomis had been arrested in Utica in 1858 for passing counterfeit money and was being held in the Utica jail. The main evidence against him was the counterfeit money itself. District Attorney Munger was supposed to prosecute the case, and evidence of Grove's guilt was overwhelming.

Munger lived in the town of Camden. Late one night, Munger was returning home after playing cards with friends. As he was crossing the village green, suddenly from the shadows two masked men emerged, placed a blanket over his head, and took his wallet. It just happened that Munger was carrying in his wallet all the counterfeit bills that were to be used as evidence against Grove at his trial. Munger said that he could not identify the men who took his wallet, and since the evidence was gone, all charges against Grove would have to be dropped. People who knew the Loomises nodded when they heard the story, as it seemed clear to them that Munger had cooperated with the Loomises to have his wallet taken and make it look like a robbery.

It was clear to everyone that if the Loomis Gang was ever going to be brought under control, Jim Filkins would have to somehow be made a law officer again. The solution was found by W. J. Bissell, the storekeeper in Waterville. Why not ask Filkins, he suggested, to move from North Brookfield to Waterville and then have a special election to elect him a constable in Waterville? Filkins agreed and moved, an election was held, and Filkins was elected without opposition to the constable position. The *Waterville Times* newspaper reported that Filkins had been "chosen to his office [as constable] because of his supposed competency to look after certain characters in our vicinity, and our citizens are determined to fully sustain him." The Loomises were furious, and Denio Loomis publicly vowed to shoot Filkins if he ever came on Loomis land again. The battle, it appeared, was not over but was just beginning.

As soon as he had been officially confirmed as constable, Jim Filkins went to work. He obtained a search warrant for the Loomis' home and arrived one afternoon with three deputies. Wash and Cornelia were the only ones at home, and they watched as Filkins and his men searched the house. They found nothing until they reached the attic, where some floorboards appeared to have been recently replaced. Prying them up they could see nothing but blackness. Filkins and one assistant went downstairs to get a candle. As soon as he did so, Wash Loomis jumped into the dark space, brought out several bags, and hid them in parts of the attic that had already been searched. Wash told the other two deputies that he would pay them well if they said nothing to Filkins.

Fortunately the deputies were honest, and when Wash returned they immediately told him what Wash had done. When the bags were opened they were found to contain revolvers, boots, shoes, lap robes, clothing, and other items that had all been stolen. Filkins immediately arrested Wash and took him to Waterville to Judge Church, who was an honest judge, to be arraigned. "Why do you bring this infernal scoundrel before me?" Judge Church asked Filkins. "Why don't you hang him?"

At Wash Loomis' hearing before Judge Church, several members of the Loomis Gang attended as spectators. Other people from the village attended, as well, including a tailor who had been robbed of several suits a few months earlier. At Wash's hearing the tailor noticed George Peckham, a member of the Loomis Gang, wearing one of the suits that had been stolen from his store. The tailor quietly went to Jim Filkins and told him, and Filkins arrested the gang member on the spot. George Peckham did not have far to go to be arraigned before Judge Church that day, since he was already in the courtroom.

Filkins returned to the Loomis' home a few days later with a new search warrant. He was determined to keep the Loomises so busy defending themselves in court that they would not have time for criminal activities. This time the warrant was to search for stolen sheep, and Filkins soon found several of them mixed in with the Loomis' own sheep. Wash pretended to be surprised at Filkins' finding, and told him that somebody else had probably brought the sheep to the Loomis farm in order to make it appear that the Loomises had stolen them. Filkins just smiled at the imaginative alibi and placed Wash under arrest once again.

Filkins continued his searches of the Loomis home, arriving every few days with a new search warrant. On one occasion, Filkins and his deputies had a warrant for Plumb Loomis' arrest, but Plumb ran for the swamp. Albert Root, one of Filkins' deputies, caught Plumb from behind, threw him to the ground, and gave him a few kicks for good measure. Pointing his revolver at Plumb, Root told him to either come along quietly or be shot.

As soon as Plumb had been released on bail he sued Root for assault. He accused Root of having badly beaten him and of pointing the revolver at his eyes. The case was heard by Judge Church in Waterville. Plumb described the beating in great detail and told Judge Church that he could even see the bullets in Root's revolver pointing at him.

Judge Church looked doubtful. He picked up the gun in question, pointed it directly at Plumb, and asked him to say whether there were bullets in it or not. Plumb hesitated a moment, then said with great confidence that no, there were no bullets in it. Judge

Church opened the revolver and let the bullets fall onto the desk. "Case dismissed," he said.

It was all becoming too much for the Loomises. They became increasingly angry as Filkins arrived with search warrant after search warrant. The Loomises were having to appear in court almost every day as more and more crimes were charged to them. Something, they all agreed, would have to be done.

It was midnight on July 22, 1863, when the Filkins family heard a knock on the back door in Waterville. Mr. and Mrs. Filkins were getting ready for bed in the single bedroom that they shared with their four young children. There had been rumors that the Loomis Gang was going to kill Filkins, so he picked up his revolver and approached the door carefully. "Who is it?" Filkins called out. "I'm Mr. Clark's hired man," a voice returned, and I've come to tell you where to find . . ."

Filkins recognized the unmistakable voice of Plumb Loomis. He stepped away from the locked door to make sure that his revolver was fully loaded. Just at that moment a barrage of bullets passed through the window, striking Filkins. Mrs. Filkins screamed as Filkins fell back. Two more blasts followed, tearing away the blinds and the lower part of the window. Filkins lay bleeding on the floor, unconscious. Neighbors saw three dark forms running away from the house.

Chapter 6

The Loomis Gang and the Civil War

Most people said that it was a miracle that Jim Filkins had not been killed. Visitors to the Filkins' home the next day counted fourteen shot holes in the mantel and forty-seven more through the bedcurtains; the bedroom door was also full of buckshot. Filkins had been hit in both arms, but Waterville's two doctors had been able to stop the bleeding. Filkins' arms were heavily bandaged, and he was told that he would not be able to use them for many weeks.

The Loomis Gang's attempt to murder Jim Filkins was a turning point in the fight against the Loomises. Up until then, most people in Waterville and surrounding towns were willing to let the law work its way against them. People assumed that if they were patient for long enough, the Loomises would eventually be put in jail.

But the attempted murder of a law officer changed things. People increasingly talked of other solutions, and usually "the California solution" was included as a possibility. This could be seen even in newspaper stories, such as in the following 1863 editorial about the Loomis Gang from the *Waterville Times*:

"For years it has been attempted to bring the gang to justice through process of law but without success. The law proving an utter failure as a means of stopping the depredations and outrages of this vile gang, and no man's life or property being safe while it is within their reach, what is to be done? We think there is but one way to go in order to put a stop to it, which is, to use the California remedy; give them so many hours in which to leave the state, and if not gone at the end of the time speci-fied, a judicious lynching."

A major reason why people were losing patience with the Loomises was the Civil War. Each day people in Waterville re-ceived letters from their sons. These young men, who had gone to fight for the Union Army, described terrible battles and the deaths of their comrades. At the Battle of Antietam, in September 1862, over 2,100 Union soldiers had been killed and 10,000 more had been injured. At Gettysburg, which had taken place just three weeks before Filkins was shot, 3,070 Union Army soldiers had died and almost 20,000 had been wounded, captured, or were missing. A regiment from Madison County had fought at Gettys-burg, and 306 of its men had been killed, wounded, or captured in a single hour during the battle.

The war was taking a terrible toll. Everyone in central New York knew a family that had lost a son in battle. At the same time, the war was causing prices to rise sharply so that items like sugar and coffee were becoming extremely expensive. With most young men off fighting, women and children were having to do most of the men's farm work, including picking the hops and other crops, which had to be harvested when they were ripe.

Because of the increasing number of deaths among Union sol-diers, President Abraham Lincoln decided early in 1863 that they must begin a draft. All men between ages twenty and forty-five would be required to join the Union Army unless they paid a fee of $300, which would allow them to not join. The draft was very un-popular, and its implementation caused riots in New York City in which over three thousand people were killed.

The Loomis family included six healthy young men, but not one of them fought for a single day in the Union Army. All their neighbors and everyone in the surrounding towns were making sacrifices for the war effort, but the Loomises were making none.

On the contrary, the Loomises appeared to be profiting from the war. This was because the Confederate Army had superior soldiers in its cavalry divisions and they repeatedly stole horses from the Union Army. In one raid alone, in October of 1862, Confederate cavalry forces stole over five hundred Union Army horses. Because of these losses the Union Army had to constantly buy new horses at increasing prices. The Loomis Gang, which specialized in stolen horses, became a major seller to the Union Army.

This became obvious in central New York in 1863 and 1864, when horse thefts increased sharply. Newspapers reported the theft of horses almost daily, and often linked them directly to the Loomis Gang. For example:

Utica Telegraph, January 30, 1863: "On Friday night last Charles Champlin's horse was stolen from the Central Hotel in Utica. Suspecting that the thief was a member of the Loomis Gang, he went to a livery and procured a fast horse and a companion and started southward (to the Loomis home)." The horse and sleigh were recovered there.

Waterville Times, May 28, 1863: "The horse which was stolen about two weeks ago from Mr. George A. Peck of Marshall has been recovered through the energy and shrewdness of Officer Filkins. The horse was stolen by two young men (who were members of the Loomis Gang)."

Lowville Journal, July 3, 1863: "The notorious Bill Loomis of Oneida County was arrested at his home last Sunday night by Deputy Sheriff Matthews of Canton, St. Lawrence County, on a charge of stealing a horse from a man in Canton. . . . Loomis made a considerable resistance when arrested, fighting until he was overcome by the superior strength of the sheriff."

Most of the horses stolen by Loomis Gang members were loaded onto boats on the Erie Canal, then taken to Albany or New York City, where they were sold to the Union Army for prices that became higher each year. And each year the Loomises became richer, profiting from the war.

In addition to not contributing any men to the Union Army while at the same time profiting from the war, the Loomises did something else that made their neighbors even more angry. Soldiers who ran away from their units were a major problem for both the Union Army and the Confederate Army during the Civil War. These men were called deserters, and approximately ten percent of all soldiers on both sides deserted. Most people had great contempt for these deserters, as well as for anyone who helped them.

The Loomis home was widely known to be a refuge for deserters. Many men who deserted were ashamed to go to their own homes so they went to the Loomis place instead and became members of the gang. Deserters from the Civil War were, in fact, the major source of new Loomis Gang members. An article in a February 1863 edition of the *Waterville Times* describing a raid by Filkins, who was looking for stolen horses, said:

> "When the loud knocking was made on the door, there was a great stamping and shuffling heard inside, and on looking in the window no less than a dozen deserters with military clothes upon them. . . . The house is evidently a rendezvous for these scamps."

On at least one occasion, Grove Loomis was arrested and charged with "concealing and employing deserters," but as usually happened, the charges were later dropped.

The Civil War had one other effect that would eventually lead to the downfall of the Loomis Gang, and this effect may have been the most important of all. The war exposed many young men to guns, violence, and the killing of other men. These young men, most of whom had been farm boys, had merely killed rabbits and deer before the war, but during the war they learned how to kill men. The war hardened them, made them accustomed to violence, and more ready to use violence again, as the Loomises would learn.

A good example of the effect of the Civil War on the young

men from the Waterville area can be seen in letters written home by Hermon Clarke, who had been a clerk in Bissell's General Store before he joined the Union Army in August 1862. Within a few months of joining, he had been exposed to destruction and death such as he had never imagined in Waterville. Here, for example, is part of his letter of December 28, 1862, written following the Battle of Fredericksburg:

"Yesterday afternoon I went over towards the Capitol to a hospital. They had just buried 14 men that died the day before. There were five in the dead house that had died since morning. There were 250 at that hospital yesterday morning from Fredericksburg, and there was a large dry goods box full of feet and hands they had taken from the wounded. That will make one homesick if anything will."

Throughout 1863 and 1864, Clarke and his fellow soldiers had to endure terrible cold in the winter, heat in the summer, inadequate food supplies, disease, and—always on the horizon—death. At the Battle of the Wilderness in Virginia in May 1864, Hermon Clarke's regiment suffered heavy losses and Clarke described in a letter home how

" . . . the battlefield took fire and burned the wounded, about 70 Rebs [Confederate soldiers] and 10 of our men. . . . I don't know how many we lost, but there were a great many wounded that we saw. I tell you it was sickening to go along the woods and see the wounded, some knocked all to pieces, some bleeding to death and suffering in every form. It was so hot that a dead man would turn black in a few hours."

Two months later, as Hermon Clarke's regiment fought with the Union Army as it moved slowly toward Richmond, the capital of the Confederacy, he wrote:

"The average killed and wounded in our Regt. [regiment] is about 4 per day. So far one out of four has been killed instantly, and there will be more than half that go to the hospital [to] die."

On August 2, 1864, he wrote:

"Sixteen from our Brigade died of sunstroke before 3 P.M., and others were severely injured by heat."

On October 3, 1864, Clarke narrowly escaped being wounded:

"There were about 275 men of our Regiment [who] went in and we lost over 120 killed, wounded and missing. . . . A spent ball hit me on the shoulder but didn't go through my blouse. A piece of shell struck my gun and broke it. The gun saved my leg."

And on October 28 Clarke's closest friend from Waterville was killed as the two fought together on the road to Richmond. Day after day the slaughter of young men continued, as described in Clarke's letter of November 13:

"Men wounded in every manner imaginable. Some dead, others dying—giving their last message to some comrade. Some cursing the war that deprived them of a leg or an arm and made them cripples for life, and in the same breath praying for their families who were suffering and, they know, must always suffer by reason of it."

In a single month the Union Army lost 60,000 men.

Meanwhile, as Hermon Clarke and other young men from Waterville and the surrounding area were dying on battlefields to the south, the Loomis Gang continued to grow rich. Central New York appeared to no longer be subject to county, state, or federal laws but only to Loomis laws. The Loomis Gang grew bolder with each passing month, and it seemed nothing would ever stop them.

This was well-illustrated in late 1864, when several residents of North Brookfield, the village situated on the other side of Nine Mile Swamp from the Loomis home, met secretly to form the North Brookfield Protective Association. The purpose of the association was to enlist prominent residents of the village to decide what to do about the Loomis Gang. Everyone was sworn to secrecy, and another meeting was scheduled to be held at the Baptist

Church a few nights later.

At the second meeting all of the important people in town were in attendance. Solutions proposed to counteract the Loomis problem varied widely, and it seemed like the North Brookfield Protective Association was finally prepared to take action. Each person present was asked to contribute one dollar toward a fund that would be used to fight the Loomises. As the money was being collected, the back door of the church opened and in walked Wash and Grove Loomis, having been tipped off. "We have heard that you are forming an organization to stop the thieving and horse stealing going on in our neighborhood," said Wash. "Grove and I think it is a fine plan and we want to join." Wash then threw two one dollar bills onto the table and the Loomis brothers walked out, laughing heartily. The participants at the meeting quickly scurried to their homes and that was the end of the Protective Association.

At the burning of the Madison County Courthouse in Morrisville on October 10, 1864, the Loomises exhibited even greater daring and arrogance. Wash, Grove and Plumb Loomis were scheduled to go to trial the next day on a variety of charges. However, the night before the trial was to begin, a fire broke out in the courthouse.

Volunteers arrived quickly, and towed the pumper from the firehouse to the courthouse. The firehose was unrolled. However, when the pumping of water began, water merely squirted out holes in the hose. On closer inspection it was evident that before the fire started, someone had gone to the firehouse and used an ax to cut the hose in several places. The hose and pumper were useless, and the fire quickly engulfed the courthouse, completely destroying it. All evidence against the Loomises was also destroyed. As a crowd of residents of Morrisville watched helplessly, Wash, Grove, and Plumb Loomis walked up and asked whether there was anything they could do to help put out the fire. Nobody in the crowd had any doubt regarding who had started the fire or who had cut the hose. But to then turn up at the fire and offer to help put it out achieved a new height of arrogance.

Slowly but surely, during late 1864 and early 1865, the Union Army pushed back the Confederates. Finally, on April 3 the Union Army entered Richmond. Five days later at nearby Appomattox Court House, the Confederate Army officially surrendered and the war was over. Joy and relief rippled across America as news of the war's end spread. Church bells in Waterville, Sangerfield, North Brookfield, and all the surrounding villages rang in celebration of the Union Army's victory and the end of the war. The Loomises heard the bells. What they did not know was that the bells would signal the end of the Loomis Gang as well.

Chapter 7

A Halloween Murder

It had been a bloody war. One out of every six soldiers who had fought in the Union Army had died. More Americans had died than would die in World War I and World War II combined. It was a rare family in upstate New York that did not know at least one young man who would never return.

And yet the killings were not quite over. On April 14, just five days after the end of the war, President Abraham Lincoln was shot to death in Washington by John Wilkes Booth, a Confederate sympathizer. The nation mourned Lincoln at the same time it celebrated the war's end. It was a strange time.

Hermon Clarke wrote to his family in Waterville describing how the war's end was celebrated by black residents in southern towns:

> "It was interesting to see the colored population. So happy a crowd I never saw: families standing on the sidewalk shouting 'We are free! We are free! Kissing one another and running to their neighbors, kissing them. The biggest thing I ever saw."

When Hermon Clarke and his regiment finally arrived at the Utica Train Station on June 18 they were greeted by a cheering crowd and by the Utica City Band playing "Home, Sweet Home." Clarke and the other soldiers from Waterville were glad to be home. But there was still one more battle to be fought. There was still the Loomis Gang.

Hermon Clarke and his friends were told by their families

about the latest rampages of the Loomis Gang. Since the end of the war two months earlier, the Loomises had launched a crime wave throughout central New York that exceeded anything they had done in the past. Robberies were reported almost every night in homes, stores, offices, factories and highway tollhouses. Anyone who tried to organize public opinion against the Loomises had their barn burned. Nobody felt safe, even in their own home.

The reason why the Loomises undertook the wave of robberies in 1865 was because the market for stolen horses had suddenly dried up. During the war the Union Army had become their best customer, and the Loomises made so much money selling stolen horses to the Army that robberies were of less importance. With the war's end, however, the Army no longer needed horses. So the Loomises returned to robberies as a means of keeping money flowing to them.

The army veterans returning from the Civil War were greeted not only by the Loomis Gang's new crime wave, but also by the fact that officers of the law were virtually helpless to stop the Loomises. In Madison County the Loomises had burned down the Madison County Courthouse in October 1864, destroying all evidence against them in a large number of cases. On the night of May 10, 1865, they also broke into the county clerk's office in Morrisville and stole all other remaining indictments against them. That same month, District Attorney Hiram T. Jenkins, having no doubt been bribed by the Loomises, announced that he had dropped all charges against them in Oneida County. Despite all their crimes, there was not a single charge remaining against the Loomis Gang in either Madison County or Oneida County. The residents of Waterville and surrounding towns were incredulous.

For Civil War veterans like Hermon Clarke and his friends, it was obvious that something had to be done. The Loomis men had not fought in the war, had handsomely profited from the war, had harbored deserters, had stolen the horses and robbed the homes of the men who had gone to fight. The time had arrived for action.

Hermon Clarke returned to his job as clerk in Bissell's General

Store. Sometime during the summer of 1865, shortly after the veterans had returned from the war, a small group of men began meeting in the storehouse above Bissell's. The group called themselves the Sangerfield Vigilantes Committee and was highly secret. They remembered what had happened to the North Brookfield Protective Association a few months earlier when Wash and Grove Loomis had walked into their meeting, effectively ending the group. This time fewer people would know, and the Loomises would not find out.

Civil War veterans like Hermon Clarke and John Garvey were members of the Vigilantes Committee. So were W. J. Bissell, Charles Green, Alexis Seymour and Morris Terry. As discussions evolved during the summer some younger men, including Morris Terry's son, Cort, and W. J. Bissell's son, Hank, were also included. And of course Constable Jim Filkins was a member. He was fully recovered from his wounds and anxious to settle the score with the men who had tried to kill him.

By the end of the summer the Vigilantes Committee had agreed upon a plan. The only remaining question was when to put it into effect. Rumors circulated about secret meetings and a secret plan, but most people did not know whether or not the rumors were true. The Loomises probably heard them as well, but they had heard such rumors before. The Loomises had never been richer, their gang had never been larger, but all indictments against them in Madison and Oneida Counties were no longer in effect. The Loomises believed that they were untouchable.

In the middle of the night on October 31, 1865, four figures moved quietly through the night toward the Loomis home. It was the time of year when cold winds blow from the west, signaling the coming of winter to Nine Mile Swamp. The trees were bare of all leaves except for occasional stragglers that had forgotten to fall. Corn stood in the field awaiting a final harvesting, while open milkweed pods shed white fingers into the night. It was Halloween. There would be tricks, but no treat.

Nobody was certain how the four men got into the Loomis

home without awakening anyone. Some people said later that a member of the Loomis Gang had been bribed to poison the dogs, but this is not certain. There were at least seventeen people sleeping in the Loomis home that night including Wash, Grove, Plumb, and Denio Loomis and seven other men who were members of the gang. The four intruders were badly outnumbered, but they had surprise on their side.

What happened next was recounted in detail by people in the house, in the *Utica Morning Herald* and again later at Jim Filkins' trial. Someone knocked loudly on Wash Loomis' window from outside and called "Wash." Wash answered, "What do you want?" The voice said, "I want to speak to you a minute," and told him to come to the back door. Wash went downstairs and suddenly there was "a dreadful jar that shook the house all over."

Immediately after, three men came up the stairs, two carrying pistols and the other a candle. They went from room to room looking carefully at the occupants of each bed. When they found Grove he was getting dressed. They took him roughly by his collar and escorted him downstairs into the back kitchen. As soon as they had closed the door one of the men began beating Grove with the butt end of his gun, hitting him several times in the head as Grove hollered "Murder! Murder!" The assailant then shot at Grove once as he was falling to the floor, but the bullet narrowly missed him. When Grove was down, one of the assailants began jumping up and down on his prone body while the other two kicked him. When they were quite certain that he was unconscious, they put some coats on him, poured kerosene onto the coats and set them afire.

Grove's cries awakened everyone in the house who was not already awake. Cornelia and Rhoda Loomis ran to the kitchen and opened the door. Seeing Grove's prone body with flames coming up, they screamed. By this time, Plumb and Denio Loomis had dressed and were coming down the stairs. Cornelia said: "Grove is dead, the house is afire, run as fast as you can." Plumb and Denio then ran out the front door and across the fields to Mr. Edward Mason's house, where they hid for several hours. The other gang members remained in their beds, apparently terrified by what was taking place.

Cornelia and Rhoda returned to the back kitchen. The men had left Grove for dead and gone outside to set the Loomis barns afire. Cornelia and Rhoda took the burning coats off Grove and threw them into the fireplace. Nellie Smith, Grove's girlfriend, then came into the room, knelt down beside Grove, and asked: "Have they killed you dead?" Grove groaned so, Nellie later said, "I knew there was life in him." His face was bloody and swollen, and one eye was blackened and swollen closed.

Incredibly, Grove revived quickly. The flames had burned the coats covering him but had not burned Grove himself. He slowly got up from the floor and complained of pain in his head and his stomach where he had been kicked. According to the account later given by Nellie Smith:

> "Grove put his hat on and went out of the northeast door; he went up to the shanty where the horse was and unlocked the door. I did not go with him. He came back and said to me: 'If you see any signs of fire run up and cut the halter and let the horse loose.'"

Grove then got a ladder to use to put out the fire in the barn, but as he did so he fell to the ground unconscious.

The cries of fire had stimulated the other gang members to finally get dressed and come downstairs. Seeing that the intruders had left, they went to work to put out the several fires that had been set. Grove slowly revived again and began to assess the situation. Cornelia said that Plumb and Denio had gone to Mr. Mason's house to hide. Everyone else seemed to be accounted for except Wash. Where was Wash?

The search for Wash did not take very long. One of the gang members found him lying unconscious and covered with blood beneath the woodhouse. His wounds were obviously severe, and his skull had been fractured in several places.

Dr. Preston was summoned from Waterville but said there was

nothing that could be done. Loomis family members sat next to Wash as life slowly ebbed from him. Early that afternoon he died. Wash Loomis, the leader of the Loomis Gang, had been murdered.

Chapter 8

A Hanging

The murder of Wash Loomis was major news throughout New York State. The *Utica Morning Herald* headline read "Startling Murder in Sangerfield." Even the *New York Times* carried a prominent story under the heading: "Mob Law in Oneida County." In Sangerfield, Waterville and all the surrounding villages, the murder was the only thing being discussed, as groups of people gathered on street corners to exchange rumors.

A formal inquest on the murder was held immediately. Officials questioned everybody who had been staying at the Loomises that night. Constable Jim Filkins was not invited to take part in the proceedings for one very good reason—everybody said that it had been he who had murdered Wash Loomis. Others who were prominently mentioned as having helped Filkins were Hank Bissell, Cort Terry, and Civil War veteran John Garvey, although nobody knew for certain. Members of the Vigilantes Committee were all completely silent about the affair, having been sworn to secrecy forever.

The evidence against Jim Filkins was in fact overwhelming. Grove, Cornelia and Rhoda Loomis as well as several gang members all asserted that they had seen Filkins there, and Grove added that it was Filkins who had both beaten him with his gun and shot at him. Filkins' handcuffs, which had accidentally fallen from his pocket, had been found at the murder scene. Part of the handle of Filkins' pistol, which had broken as he was beating Grove, was also found there. Nobody had any doubt who had killed Wash

Loomis, and most people believed that Jim Filkins was headed to jail, a law officer who had broken the law.

But most people were wrong. They did not consider the skill of Roscoe Conkling, then a United States Congressman who spent much of the year in Washington, D.C. Conkling still practiced law in Utica when Congress was not in session, and he came immediately to Filkins' assistance. Conkling remembered the role the Loomises had played fifteen years earlier in getting him voted out of office. Now was an opportunity to settle that score. Conkling also admired Filkins for the way he had stood up to the Loomises when nobody else had dared to do so.

On November 18, 1865, less than three weeks after the murder of Wash Loomis, Jim Filkins was indicted by a grand jury in Utica on charges of murder, assault with intent to kill, and arson. District Attorney Hiram Jenkins, an old friend of the Loomises, asked that Filkins be held without bail until he could be brought to trial. The Loomises had tried many times to get Filkins jailed, and this time they believed they had succeeded. Conkling, however, argued strongly that Filkins would represent no danger to the community if he were freed on bail and guaranteed that he would not run away. Conkling's arguments convinced the judge, and four days later he was released from jail on ten thousand dollars bail. The money was collected from twenty-eight of Waterville's leading citizens as a gesture of united support for Filkins.

The Loomises were outraged. Not only had Jim Filkins killed Wash, but he was also out on bail after only four days. Grove Loomis let it be known that he would pay any man who would kill Filkins one thousand dollars. One evening shortly thereafter, three Loomis gang members walked into the Park Hotel in Waterville and announced that they had come to kill Filkins. When Filkins, unarmed, entered the hotel a few minutes later, the three drew their guns but did not shoot. Filkins turned, calmly walked out of the hotel to go to his house and get his gun. When he returned to the hotel, the three men were gone.

Despite Wash Loomis' death, the other family members were

determined to carry on without him. In fact, they had been involved in stealing, counterfeiting and other illegal activities for so long that Rhoda Loomis and her grown children could not imagine doing anything else. Crime was not only a way of life for the Loomis family; it was the only life they had ever known.

Robberies and thefts resumed in central New York in late November. One such robbery was planned for December 6 against Dennison Crandall, a farmer who lived near Leonardsville, ten miles from the Loomis farm. Crandall was rumored to keep large amounts of money at his home, and on December 5, the Loomises were told, he had withdrawn over two thousand dollars from the bank.

At sundown on December 6, three masked members of the Loomis Gang approached Crandall's farmhouse. While one stood guard outside, the other two, armed with pistols, entered the house, and demanded that Mr. Crandall give them his money. Crandall told them to get out, whereupon one of the robbers picked up a piece of firewood and swung it at him. Crandall was sixty-five years old but was still strong. According to a newspaper account, Crandall then

" . . . leaped forward and landed a stiff blow to the outlaw's stomach. While the robber clutched at his middle, Crandall seized him and tripped him, throwing him to the floor. The other masked man drew his pistol, but Crandall hit him with a chunk of wood, until he dropped to the floor. The first outlaw, having recovered from the blow to his stomach, leaped on Crandall, but the farmer threw him aside like a sack of wheat, got him on his back and hit him wildly with his hands. The second outlaw joined the fray and, as Crandall rose to meet him, the first outlaw drew his pistol and fired. The farmer staggered as the ball lodged behind his ear. The two outlaws leaped on him and bore him to the floor. Blood streamed down the side of his face. 'Let me go,' he panted, 'and I will get you some money.' He broke loose, ran into his bedroom and slammed the door behind him. Though the room was in darkness, his hands found what they were searching for, a long flail stick which he had nicknamed his 'headache stick.' The door was pushed open slightly and a pistol was thrust into the room. Crandall struck the hand with his stick. He swung the door open to face the burning eyes of the first outlaw. He raised his stick to ward off an attack, but the stick caught on the door-casing. The outlaw raised his pistol and fired point-blank at Crandall's face. Though the ball struck the farmer slightly below the eye, he did not fall, but advanced toward the outlaws, who retreated toward the stove. At this moment a third masked man appeared in the kitchen. Coolly, he raised his pistol and shot Crandall through the back of the head. As the aged farmer staggered across the room and fell headlong, his wife screamed. The outlaw shot her, too."

Incredibly, Dennison Crandall was not dead, and he regained consciousness two hours later. Although he had been hit by three bullets and was covered with blood, he managed to walk a half mile to his brother's house. The newspaper said that "his footsteps could be traced by his blood the whole distance," and when his brother opened the door he did not recognize him. Crandall's wife was dead. The *Utica Morning Herald* called Mrs. Crandall's murder "one of the most atrocious and revolting murders that was ever perpetrated in the county."

Community reaction to the murder of Mrs. Crandall was outrage. Although it could not be proven, most people assumed that it was the work of the Loomis Gang. People had assumed that with Wash dead, the Loomis Gang would no longer be a menace. It was becoming increasingly clear that this assumption was wrong. And on the street corners of Waterville, people in hushed voices were saying that something more would have to be done.

Shortly after the Crandall murder, the Loomises again came to public attention. Passing counterfeit money had always been a Loomis Gang activity, and in early 1866 counterfeit bills began flooding the community. Jim Filkins heard a rumor that the Loomises had received a large delivery of those bills from New York City, so he decided to investigate. The fact that he was under indictment for the murder of Wash Loomis and awaiting trial led some people to say that he should not be acting as constable, but nobody else wanted the job, so he was allowed to do so.

Filkins took six men with him for the raid, suspecting quite correctly that he might not be welcomed at the Loomis home. Just two months previously he had, after all, murdered Wash and tried to murder Grove. That kind of activity does not usually make a person welcome. When they arrived at the Loomis home, Rhoda Loomis and Cornelia were the only ones there, and they received Filkins with surprising cordiality. Rhoda invited the men to search wherever they wished, and even offered them beer from a new keg. After drinking several beers, Filkins' men were feeling good and rapidly lost interest in the counterfeit money. As they sat drinking, Filkins noticed that the beer keg was oddly shaped. He took it outside and split it with an ax, finding a false bottom on the keg, packed with counterfeit bills. A further search turned up several more beer kegs, also with counterfeit bills. Rhoda and Cornelia Loomis were immediately arrested and taken to Utica for a court hearing.

Throughout the winter and spring of 1866 the members of the Loomis Gang continued their activities. Despite repeated raids by Filkins, there appeared to be no slowing them down. The Vigilantes Committee resumed secret meetings in the storeroom over Bissell's store in Waterville, and members of the committee traveled to Madison, Morrisville, Hamilton, and other surrounding towns to meet with like-minded citizens. Everyone agreed that *something* more was needed to combat the Loomis Gang, and this time the solution should be a more permanent one.

An official report on the Loomis Gang was also released by the New York State Prison Association. The report received wide publicity in newspapers throughout the state and was eventually covered by a newspaper in London. It began:

"There is a family residing in Oneida County who, according to common fame, have followed the profession of thieving for nearly twenty years. They have grown rich by their unlawful practices. . . . These men have been indicted times without number, but none of them have every been convicted, nor have any of them ever been in jail for a longer time than was sufficient for a bondsman to arrive at the prison."

The Loomis Gang had indeed become famous, or rather, infamous.

If people still had any doubt that additional action would be needed against the Loomises, those doubts were put to rest by the events of June 10. Filkins had received word that Bill Alvord, one of the most notorious members of the gang, was at the Loomis home, and Filkins had several outstanding warrants for his arrest. Filkins arrived at the Loomises with five other men just as dawn was breaking. They were met by Rhoda, who shouted up the stairs to warn everyone that Filkins had come.

Filkins and his men climbed up the stairs to the second floor, only to find that several members of the Loomis Gang had climbed into the attic. Filkins' group started cautiously up those stairs, but one of the gang members at the top of the attic stairs said, "Go back, or I will shoot you through!" One of Filkins' men advanced further but was suddenly hit on the head with the butt end of a gun. Filkins shot, striking him twice.

A gunfight ensued, spilling down the stairs and into the yard. Filkins was hit by bullets twice, one of them breaking his arm and the other knocking him unconscious. Two other men with Filkins were also injured, and two large pigs, a horse, and a cow were killed in the shootout before it was over. Filkins' men loaded him into a wagon and took him to Waterville to be treated.

Although Filkins and his men did not know it at the time, one of the men in the attic was Bill Alvord, and it was he who had shot Filkins. However, in the gunfight Alvord had also been seriously wounded. The Loomises knew that Filkins' men would return shortly with reinforcements, and so they had to get Alvord safely away. Since the roads from the Loomis home were being watched, Rhoda Loomis disguised the injured Alvord as a woman by dressing him in a dress and bonnet, and Grove Loomis drove him away past the unsuspecting lawmen.

In the week following the shootout at the Loomis home, the Vigilantes Committee met several times. Messengers went back and forth to all the surrounding towns, and it was clear to everyone that something was going to happen. The Loomises undoubtedly heard the rumors, but there was not much they could do.

On Saturday afternoon, June 16, groups of armed men began to gather in Peterboro, Canastota, Oneida, Morrisville, Madison and Hamilton. In Waterville the village was strangely quiet, except for Bissell's General Store, where men came and went quickly and talked in hushed tones. It was a fine summer day for planting crops, yet few farmers could be seen in the fields of Madison and southern Oneida Counties. Jokingly, they told each other that it was a day for harvesting instead.

As dusk descended, the men left their villages and started toward the Loomis home. Many of them had had horses or sheep stolen by the Loomises, and a few had had their homes or businesses robbed or their barns burned. Their weapons included firearms of all descriptions, a keg of gunpowder and a thick rope. Many of the men were veterans of the Civil War, and they exchanged stories of the war experiences as they rode along. The leadership of the groups included virtually every law officer from Madison County who was not thought to be on the Loomises' payroll, and many from Oneida County as well. Jim Filkins was still recovering from his gunshot wounds of the previous week, so he could not join the group. It was the night he had worked for eight years to bring about, and lying in his bed in Waterville he must have been pleased.

By the middle of the night, the men had met at a prearranged site one mile from the Loomises' place. From there they walked silently to the house and surrounded it. Rhoda Loomis spotted them first, more than one hundred of them on all sides of the house, with guns leveled at the windows. Grove, Plumb, and Cornelia were all at home, along with gang members John Stoner, John Smith, and assorted girlfriends. Vastly outnumbered, they surrendered without a fight.

Everyone was herded into the yard. Several men then went into the house, and almost immediately smoke was seen coming out of a window. Rhoda and Cornelia ran into the house and threw water on the flames, but fires had been set in other rooms, and the house was soon ablaze. Determined to save what they could, Rhoda and Cornelia carried several pieces of furniture out the front door and put them on the grass. As soon as they returned inside, the men carried the furniture around to the side of the house and threw it back into the rapidly increasing flames. Rhoda then attempted to save several gallon jugs of maple syrup and honey, handing them out the door to the men and asking them to put them on the ground. They did so, smashing each jug in the process.

Talk then turned to what to do with the Loomises. Suggestions were plentiful, including putting them back into the burning house, or putting them into the shed with the keg of gunpowder and blowing them up. Finally, Deputy Sheriff Asa Stone of Madison County took charge and ordered gang member John Stoner to be brought to the maple tree in front of the house. A thick rope was thrown over a limb and a noose fastened around Stoner's neck. As the crowd cheered, Stoner was raised off the ground and suspended for a few seconds. When he was lowered, he indicated a willingness to tell everything he knew, including the fact that it had indeed been Bill Alvord who had shot Filkins the previous week.

Plumb Loomis was brought forward next. He was probably the most disliked member of the family, and the crowd cheered heartily as the noose was put around his neck. Plumb expected to be killed by the mob, and he was determined to die bravely. When asked what he had to say for himself, he said: "If I confess you'll kill me, and if I don't confess you'll kill me, so kill me anyway."

Plumb was suspended from the ground until his tongue protruded from his mouth and his eyes looked like they were going to pop out of their sockets. The men lowered Plumb to the ground, where he lay purple-faced, gasping for breath. "Are you ready to talk now?" they asked him. Plumb refused to answer, so he was again suspended. His body twitched, then went limp. Rhoda

Loomis fell to her knees and said, "I've never prayed before, but I'm going to pray now." Shadows cast by the house, now fully ablaze, cast an eerie glow over the crowd.

When they lowered Plumb the second time, he lay limply on the ground without moving. A bucket of water was brought and thrown on him, whereupon he slowly regained consciousness. "What do you know about the Crandall murder?" he was asked. "I don't know nothing about it," Plumb answered sullenly. He was therefore suspended a third time, and went limp immediately. When he was finally lowered, he appeared to be dead. One of the men put his ear to Plumb's chest and smiled grimly. Plumb was still alive, he said. More water was brought, but Plumb came to very slowly. This time he answered more willingly. "Spare our lives," Plumb pleaded, "and we will strive henceforth to be honest, peaceful, law-abiding citizens."

Grove was brought forward next, and the noose was placed around his neck. His face was pale, and his usual arrogance was nowhere to be seen. "You saw what happened to Plumb," said the Deputy Sheriff. "If you don't want a sample of the same, you had better talk." Grove did talk, as rapidly as he could, and told the men everything they asked. He blamed most of the crimes on other gang members. "We can't be blamed for what the men who hung around here have done. If you will give us the chance, we will help you bring them to justice. We will no longer harbor outlaws and criminals."

The crowd then seemed satisfied, having heard confessions by the Loomises. After some discussion, it was decided to take Plumb to jail on an outstanding warrant and to give the other family members thirty days to be gone from the area or they "would forfeit their lives." As the men drifted away, the Loomises were left sitting by the roadside with nothing left but the clothes they had on. The house, barns, shed, and even the hophouse were all burning, the flames fanned by a brisk wind. As the sun rose, it cast its morning light on the end of the Loomis Gang.

Epilogue

The Loomises were not gone from the area at the end of thirty days, but they never recovered from that June night. Most of their money and their possessions had gone up in flames. They did not have enough money to pay Plumb's bail, so he remained in jail for several months. They could not even pay the property taxes that were due on their land so, in January 1867, most of their land was sold. Denio Loomis continued to steal from time to time, but his activities were but a mere shadow of what had once been the Loomis Gang.

The trial of Jim Filkins for the murder of Wash Loomis finally took place in June 1867, in the Rome Courthouse. Roscoe Conkling defended Filkins. Conkling had just been elected a United States Senator from New York State, but he had forgotten neither his hatred of the Loomises nor his obligation to Filkins. Conkling put on a brilliant defense and persuaded the judge to set aside Filkins' indictment on technical grounds. The Loomises were furious, but there was nothing they could do.

Filkins retired as constable and moved to Utica, where he worked as a night watchman for several years. In 1892 he became sick and returned to Waterville, where he died at the age of sixty-eight. He was buried at the cemetery at North Brookfield. His grave sits on a hillside overlooking Nine Mile Swamp, and from his grave one can clearly see the site of the Loomis farm. Jim Filkins is still keeping watch.

Roscoe Conkling became one of the most powerful politicians

in Washington. In 1876 he was a candidate to become the Republican nominee for President but lost the nomination to Rutherford B. Hayes. In 1881 Conkling resigned from the Senate and retired to live in New York City. In 1888 he developed an abscess of his ear, which spread to his brain, and he died. His grave is in Forest Lawn Cemetery in Utica. "Roscoe Conkling Park," overlooking the city of Utica, was named for him.

The Loomises continued to live in the area but caused few problems. Calista, Lucia, and of course Wash had died by 1866, and then Charlotte died in 1870. Grove settled into a small house at the edge of Nine Mile Swamp, where he lived until he died in 1878. Just before dying, he called for a minister and asked for forgiveness. At Grove's funeral, the minister said: "I have no doubt that Mr. Loomis is in Heaven with the angels. There are many evil people who have been floated to Heaven at the eleventh hour of forgiveness. I've heard some men say, 'If I've got to go and live with that crowd, I might as well be in Hell.'"

Denio was the next to go. While awaiting trial for stealing a horse in 1876, he suffered a stroke that partially paralyzed him. A second stroke followed in 1879, and finally in 1880, at the age of just forty-three, he died. Cornelia and Mrs. Rhoda Loomis settled in a small house at Hastings Center, north of Syracuse, where Rhoda died in 1887. She was ninety-five years old and had outlived eight of her twelve children. Six years later, Cornelia died following a stroke, and in 1896, Bill Loomis also died.

That left only Plumb and Wheeler Loomis alive. Plumb had bought back a few acres of Loomis land and had built a small cabin on top of the hill behind the old Loomis home. He became a local character of sorts, and could often be found drinking in the American Hotel in Waterville. On one occasion he encountered Jim Filkins at the hotel and said: "Jim, come and have a drink. You murdered my brother . . . but come and have a drink anyway." Plumb enjoyed showing off the scars on his neck caused by his hangings. One day Patrick Doyle, an Irishman, boasted to Plumb that he had helped hold the rope that hung him. Plumb replied that "while he might have deserved hanging, he would never go low enough to deserve hanging at the hands of an Irishman." In 1903, at the age of sixty-nine, Plumb Loomis died.

Wheeler Loomis was the last of the Loomis family alive, but he had been living in Ontario since 1863, when he fled New York State to avoid going to jail. In Ontario he became a respectable farmer, and most of his neighbors did not know of his criminal background. On March 20, 1911, Wheeler Loomis, age eighty, died of cancer, and his body was returned to central New York for burial. Today Wheeler Loomis' gravestone is the only one that can be found in the Sangerfield cemetery. All of the other Loomises except Bill are buried there as well, but their gravestones have fallen into decay or been removed.

The ruins of the Loomis home are still visible today, including some burned timbers and the remains of a fireplace. A path leading uphill through the woods shows terracing and drainage ditches that were dug by the Loomises. At the top of the hill is a plateau that overlooks Nine Mile Swamp. From that plateau, one can see for miles down the road leading to Sangerfield and Waterville, the road Jim Filkins and his men would ride when coming to raid the Loomises. And on a nice day, if you look carefully in the distance, you can almost see them coming.

Glossary

Some words commonly used in the nineteenth century are used less frequently now. Examples of such words used in this story are the following:

accomplice: a partner in a crime

buckshot: a large type of lead shot used in guns

constable: a type of policeman

counterfeiting: to make fake money with the intent of using it illegally as real money

draft: the taking of men for compulsory military service

hops: a plant once widely grown in New York State used to make beer

inquest: an official investigation of a death, often held before a jury

jackknife: a pocketknife

lynching: hanging a person without a trial, usually done by a mob of men

scamp: a rascal or criminal

scythe: an instrument with a long, curving blade used to cut grass or hay

tavern: a bar, saloon, or inn where alcoholic beverages are sold

About the author

Dr. Torrey grew up in Clinton, New York, just fourteen miles from the Loomis homestead, and for one summer worked on a job building a road adjacent to Nine Mile Swamp. He was educated at Princeton, McGill, and Stanford Universities, and served in the Peace Corps in Ethiopia. He is the author of sixteen books, including *Surviving Schizophrenia*, *Nowhere To Go*, *The Freudian Fraud*, *Out of the Shadows* and *Frontier Justice*. *The Roots of Treason: Ezra Pound and the Secret of St. Elizabeths* was nominated by the National Book Critics Circle as one of the five best biographies of 1983. He is a clinical and research psychiatrist and advocate for individuals with serious mental illnesses and has appeared on Donahue, Oprah, Geraldo, 60 Minutes, 20/20, and other programs. His home is now in Washington, D.C.